Masculinity, Bullying, and Aggression

A Guy's Guide

A Young Man's Guide to Contemporary Issues™

Masculinity, Bullying, and Aggression

A Guy's Guide

Sam Navarre

ROSEN PUBLISHING
New York

S

Published in 2012 by The Rosen Publishing Group, Inc.
29 East 21st Street, New York, NY 10010

First Edition

Library of Congress Cataloging-in-Publication Data

Navarre, Sam.
Masculinity, bullying, and aggression: a guy's guide/Sam Navarre.—1st ed.
p. cm.—(A young man's guide to contemporary issues)
Includes bibliographical references and index.
ISBN 978-1-4488-5525-4 (library binding)
1. Masculinity—Juvenile literature.
2. Bullying—Juvenile literature.
3. Aggressiveness—Juvenile literature. I. Title.
BF692.5.N38 2012
155.5'32—dc22

2011013572

Manufactured in the United States of America

CPSIA Compliance Information: Batch #W12YA: For further information, contact Rosen Publishing, New York, New York, at 1-800-237-9932.

Contents

A boy reads from the Torah, or Hebrew Scripture, at his Bar Mitzvah. In this Jewish coming-of-age ritual, thirteen-year-old boys take their place as men in the congregation.

INTRODUCTION

All boys will experience it at some point: they start to notice hair on their upper lip. Their voices drop. Their muscles develop. They grow hair on their chests. Slowly but surely, their bodies mature. But physical changes are only one part of growing up. Becoming a man means much more than that.

How does a boy know that he's finally become a man? Boys come of age in different ways in different cultures. Jewish boys around the world must prove that they can

read from the Torah and interpret it in front of their congregation. In the Hamar tribe in Ethiopia, a boy must run back and forth across the backs of a line of cattle to officially enter manhood. On Pentecost Island in the South Pacific, men prove their bravery by "land diving"—leaping off a wooden platform as tall as 100 feet (30.5 meters), with only a vine tied to one leg.

In North American culture, there is no single mark to measure the transition to manhood. In fact, we don't even share a single definition of manhood. Some North Americans believe that being a man means being strong and silent, never feeling any pain, disappointment, or sadness. Others insist that real men are strong enough to show their emotions. Many people maintain that a man must be physically tough and aggressive, ready to fight for respect and honor. Others disagree, saying that a real man never has to resort to violence.

Being a man in North America might mean never crying, or crying freely; being powerful, or being sensitive; pushing yourself, or acting like a slob; being chivalrous, or being crass; or acting like a perfect gentleman, or acting out as a bad boy. With so many mixed messages, it's a wonder that any guy figures out how to become a man.

But if adults in our culture have many different definitions of manhood, most boys seem to agree how a boy should act. There's an unspoken set of rules about how they should act, look, sound, and treat others. Dr. William S. Pollack, author of the book *Real Boys: Rescuing Our Sons from the Myths of Boyhood*, calls this set of rules the Boy Code.

All boys want to feel like they are manly. And most boys go far out of their way to prove their masculinity. This is a natural and normal part of growing up. But sometimes boys go a little overboard in their efforts to uphold the Boy Code. For instance, some boys try so hard to appear tough that they actually become violent.

According to the National Center for Education Statistics, 31 percent of students in grades nine to twelve reported being in a physical fight at least once in 2009. In addition, 4 percent of males said they had been in a fight twelve or more times, compared to 1 percent of females.

There are also other reasons why boys get aggressive and violent. Some boys live in violent neighborhoods, where they feel they need to defend themselves in order to survive. Other boys use violence because they don't know how else to express themselves. Our society pressures men to stifle their negative emotions in hopes that they will simply go away. But when you ignore strong feelings like sadness, anger, and shame, you only make them stronger. Sometimes these unexpressed feelings boil over and drive boys to become violent.

Boys need to realize that they can be safe and strong without resorting to violence. Perhaps more important, boys need to realize that all violence comes from a place of pain—and that when they hurt others, they are also hurting themselves.

This book intends to point out ways for boys to break free of dependence on violence, to draw strength from their emotions, and to define for themselves what it means to be a man.

You will become a man one day. But the kind of man you will become is up to you.

CHAPTER 1

Aggression: The Measure of a Man?

Feelings of aggression and competition are normal for boys. Unfortunately, our culture sometimes sends the signal that men are only men if they act aggressively—if they intimidate and threaten others, fight, or express their emotions through violence.

The Measure of a Man

Our culture has no single definition of manhood, no rite that boys must go through in order to become men. However, North American boys have some pretty strong ideas about what is manly and what is not.

Imagine that we draw a box. Inside, we'll list all of the personality traits and physical attributes that a man is supposed to have according to the Boy Code. We'll write everything a man is not supposed to be outside the box.

How is a man supposed to look? Inside the box we would list "muscular," "strong," "athletic," and "handsome."

In any culture, boys must prove that they are worthy to be considered men. In today's America, boys must also decide what being a man means to them.

Outside the box we would write such words as "frail," "effeminate," and "bookish."

How is a man supposed to sound? Inside the box we might write "low voice" and "commanding." What is he supposed to talk about? We might list "sports," "politics," or "business" inside the box. Outside the box we might write "feelings," "disappointments," and "fears." What is a male supposed to do for fun? Inside the box we might put "football." Outside the box we might put "ballet."

Dance can demand just as much strength, athleticism, discipline, and competitive spirit as sports. For many boys, pursuing the goal of becoming a dancer takes real guts and determination.

According to our culture, a man is supposed to be brave, responsible, energetic, strong, and popular with the ladies. He is not supposed to be weak, effeminate, a "sissy," or a "crybaby."

Are the categories inside and outside the box absolute? Of course not. *Billy Elliot*, the movie and Broadway show, is the story of a young boy growing up in a coal-mining town. He courageously stands up to ridicule when he decides to follow his dream of becoming a ballet dancer. He bravely pursues his goal instead of giving in to pressure from friends and family, who want him to follow the Boy Code.

Generally, our culture rewards those who fit the profile of a so-called real man with respect, honor, and acceptance. Our culture often punishes those who don't fit into the box with bullying, teasing, name-calling, and sometimes much worse.

Thinking Outside the Box

Most boys spend a lot of time—more time than they would like to admit—trying to fit inside the box. This is true of the most delicate artist and the beefiest athlete. Boys often censor or hide parts of themselves and pretend to have interests and strengths they may not possess, just to fit into our culture's ideal of manhood.

The truth is, nobody really fits inside the "real man" box. If you stayed inside the box for your whole life, you would become an emotionless robot. But human beings—including men and boys—do have emotions. If boys don't allow themselves to feel anything, they damage themselves emotionally and mentally. Ignored and repressed emotions will find other forms of expression—perhaps in depression, perhaps in violence or bullying.

What Is Aggression?

The dictionary defines aggression as "hostile or violent behavior or attitudes toward another; readiness to attack or confront." When someone goes looking for a fight, without any provocation, we say that he is being aggressive. The person who does this is known as the aggressor. These words come from the Latin *aggredi*, meaning "to attack."

Sometimes aggression is dramatic: throwing a punch or hurling a chair across a room. There are simpler, subtler forms of aggression, too. When boys "bodycheck" each other in the hallway at school, slamming their shoulders into each other, it is a form of aggression. Even friendly wrestling can be a form of aggression. In fact, innocent play is sometimes misunderstood as harmful aggression.

WHAT IF I DON'T FIT INSIDE THE BOX?

Some boys have an easier time conforming to the Boy Code than others. The captain of the football team fits more easily "inside the box" than the sensitive boy who wants to be a painter. Boys who are artistic or intellectual, who are physically different from their classmates, or who have interests that might be considered "unmanly" can sometimes have a hard time fitting in. Boys who are questioning their sexual orientation face a special challenge.

Just because the Boy Code exists doesn't mean that you have to live by it. You are a unique individual forging your own path through life. You don't have to conform to others' expectations. How you look, how you act, and what you do is up to you. It is healthier, more rewarding, more challenging, and more courageous to embrace and accept your true self than to force yourself to fit someone else's idea of masculinity.

Around the world, every culture believes that real men are courageous and strong. Well, there's nothing more courageous than being yourself when you know that some people may reject you. Being true to the person you really are is not easy. There are plenty of soldiers, firefighters, and sports stars that are terrified to honestly reveal their true selves. Strange as it may sound, you could become an example for others by being yourself so that others can see the possibilities.

You can also be aggressive without using your body at all. When you call someone else names, with the intent to embarrass or hurt the person, that's aggressive. Other forms of aggression include purposefully excluding somebody from a group, putting someone down, pulling a mean prank, giving someone the silent treatment, or writing a nasty comment on someone's Facebook wall.

Positive Aggression

Aggression in itself is not bad. All people have aggressive impulses: they allow us to protect ourselves from attack and to fight boldly for things that are important to us. For example, aggression is a vital tool when fighting a war or defending oneself. Competitive arenas such as sports,

Your aggressive impulses can drive you to succeed on the basketball court, football field, or in any other athletic arena that requires effort and determination.

business, or chess also involve a certain amount of aggression.

However, if you don't learn to control your aggressive urges and use them appropriately, they can be dangerous. You might hurt others who don't deserve to be hurt and get in trouble yourself. Controlling your aggression is not the same thing as pretending that you are never angry or never feel aggressive. Denying your anger and aggression can harm your health, depress you, and distance you from other people.

Aggression and Masculinity

In our culture, being aggressive is often identified as a masculine trait. Boys learn that if they are aggressive on the football field or basketball court, they will earn respect. According to the Boy Code, boys are supposed to be physical, and girls are supposed to be emotional. If boys cry, or discuss their feelings too honestly, they run the risk of being considered weak or girly.

When it comes to expressing negative feelings—feelings like anger, hurt, shame, and frustration—boys face a harsh choice. Society tells boys that a man should be strong and stoic (indifferent to emotions), able to "take" insults and punches without getting hurt. Many boys would rather express anger by behaving aggressively than admit feeling hurt. These boys know that going on an angry rampage might get them in trouble. However, at least they will get in trouble for being too aggressive, which is seen as manly. They think their aggression might inspire peers to respect, or at least fear, them.

The Cost of Violence

If you are aggressive or violent at school, you will definitely get in trouble, and you might even be suspended or expelled. If you mess with the wrong person, you could face retribution or vengeance from your victim or from his friends or relatives.

More important, when you resort to violence, you are hurting someone. Knowing that you caused someone else pain can make you feel guilty. Some men respond to guilt by taking a look in the mirror and deciding to change. Others try to deny that they feel guilty and make excuses for their own behavior. As a result, they become more likely to use violence again in the future.

If you start using violence to get what you want as a young man, you'll start a bad pattern that might be hard to break later in life. Have you ever heard the saying, "When all you have is a hammer, every problem looks like a nail"? Boys who solve all of their problems with aggression or violence may one day become violent with their families, engaging in domestic abuse of wives or children.

Violence and aggressive behavior are seldom the best way to get what you want. Threatening others with violence might give you a temporary sense of power, but this can transform into paranoia that your friends will turn on you. When someone is scared of you, he or she cannot really be your friend. Even if you succeed in intimidating or bullying others into giving you what you want, they will help you out of resentment and fear, not respect.

The Culture of Aggression

Young men ages eighteen to twenty-four are one of the most prized demographics among businesses. Young men spend a lot of money on movies, video games, sporting events, music, and going out with friends. For this reason,

When boys don't learn how to control their aggressive impulses, they act out in ways that get them in trouble at school, at home, or in the street.

an entire segment of our popular culture is aimed specifically at young men.

Hollywood and advertisers alike know that young men love the rush of adrenaline that comes when they watch intense competition or violence. Sports like football, hockey, wrestling, boxing, and mixed martial arts celebrate aggression. Rap and rock music often feature aggressive rhythms and violent lyrics. Hollywood blockbusters lure teenage boys with action sequences full of spectacular explosions and extreme blood and gore. First-person shooter video games let boys indulge violent fantasies as they gun down anonymous digital enemies.

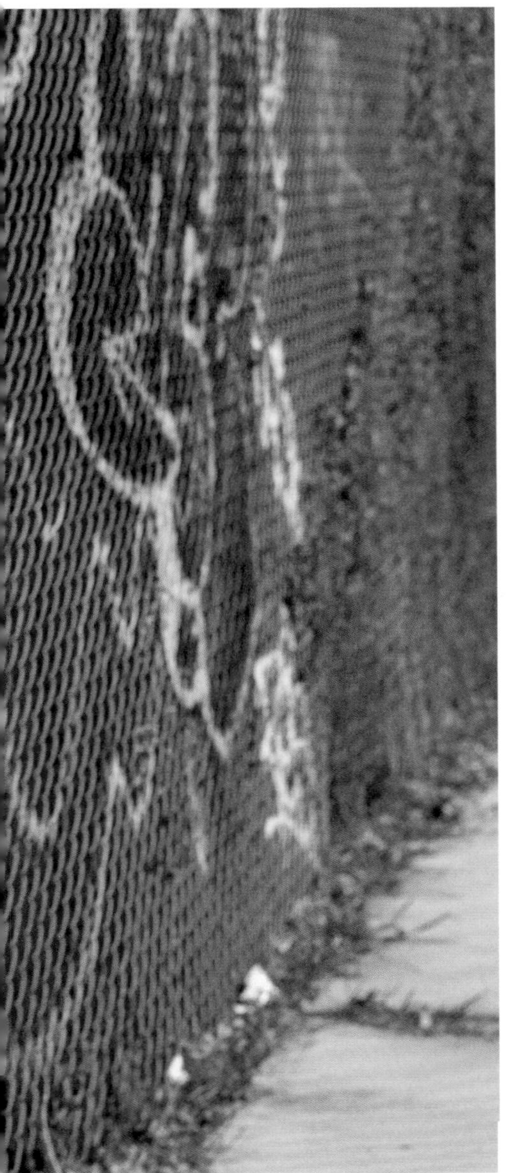

When boys are surrounded by violent images, they can become desensitized to violence. They can also develop an extreme view of what it means to be masculine and tough.

Male Subcultures

Every boy wants to belong, to feel like a vital part of a community of men that he respects and admires. Many boys seek acceptance and security inside a subculture.

A subculture is a small cultural group within a larger culture. Our society includes many male subcultures that encourage aggression. In fact, in some male subcultures, violence is the price of entrance, the sign of belonging, and the penalty for leaving.

College fraternities often require their young pledges (boys hoping to join the fraternity) to endure a form of ritual humiliation and violence called hazing. Older fraternity brothers subject the pledges to physical or emotional torture to prove their loyalty to the fraternity. The pledges look forward to the day when they can turn around and haze younger pledges themselves.

Gangs have their own rituals for testing and initiating new members. Many gangs "jump in" their new recruits, which means beat them up. Once boys join a gang, they must be ready to follow orders, which may include acting out violently, even lethally, against the gang's enemies. In many gangs, any member who wants to get out must first endure a brutal beating from the group—"blood in, blood out."

So many aspects of our popular culture, including male subcultures, tell boys that being aggressive is fundamentally, quintessentially male. Is it any surprise that boys get the message that in order to be real men, they must be aggressive?

HOMOPHOBIA

Homophobia is prejudice against gay, bisexual, and transgendered people. Unfortunately, homophobia is a big part of the Boy Code. Among many groups of boys, "gay" is a common insult. The funny thing is that most of the time, when boys call something "gay," they don't actually mean that it is homosexual. Boys often use "gay" to mean feminine, girly, or lame—the opposite of masculine. Of course, plenty of boys, gay and straight, are teased for supposedly being homosexual. Enduring homophobic taunts is a very painful experience for any boy.

Antigay slurs can be especially hurtful to boys who are attracted to other boys—especially during the adolescent years. These boys get the message that their sexual orientation is somehow wrong and that they were born defective. Some boys are so terrified of their own homosexuality that they bully, tease, or even attack other boys for supposedly being gay. These boys might hope to prove to themselves that they aren't really gay.

The oppression and repression that gay youth often suffer is deeply sad. There is nothing wrong with being gay. Homosexuals are not inherently wrong, dirty, or lame. Hiding the truth about who you are doesn't work any better than bottling up your emotions and hoping they go away.

If it is safe for you to be open about your sexual orientation, try to live honestly. It is much healthier to embrace who you really are than to live a lie. If it is not safe for you to tell others about your orientation right now, at least admit the truth to yourself. One day you will grow up, and you can seek out others who will understand and accept you.

Coming out about your sexual orientation takes strength, courage, conviction, and resilience—all very traditional masculine virtues.

The Dark Side of Masculinity

Our culture's ideals of manhood can have negative effects—on boys who sense that they will never fit the profile of a "real man," as well as on boys who try too hard to measure up to society's standards.

In trying to live up to the ideal of the strong, silent man, many boys attempt to ignore their emotions. However, this strategy never works. The longer you repress a feeling, or force yourself to hold it in, the stronger it can become. For some males, all the negative emotions they refuse to feel accumulate over time and slowly poison their lives. Men who deny all their feelings can develop an explosive temper—or fall into a deep depression. They might grow numb to the world and be unable to feel anything, good or bad. Some men become unable to recognize and share the feelings of others, making it difficult for them to form close friendships or fall in love.

The Boy Code encourages boys to be competitive with each other and always strive to be the best. This can be a great thing if competition helps inspire you to excellence. But some boys take competitive feelings too far. If they lose an athletic game, do badly on a test, or fail to measure up to others, they feel frustration and shame. They might even

Friends who accept you as you truly are, and who listen to your problems, can help you get through your teenage years unscathed.

start to label themselves "losers" or hate themselves. This type of self-loathing is dangerous, lonely, and unnecessary. When boys refuse to talk about their feelings of shame, locking them away inside, the situation is only made worse. Admitting and expressing feelings of disappointment is the first step to moving past them.

It's important to realize that nobody lives up to the standard of the ideal man. Nobody fits perfectly into the box. To be a complete, healthy human being, sometimes you need to think outside the box.

Bullying

Unfortunately, bullying is a fact of life for many kids. In fact, bullying is so common that many adults treat bullying like it's no big deal. If they see a boy bullying classmates, they might excuse him by saying, "Boys will be boys." They might sympathize with a boy who is being bullied but advise him to just toughen up.

These attitudes ignore just how dangerous and destructive bullying can be. Young victims of bullying may become depressed, neglect their schoolwork, withdraw from friends, and even have thoughts about suicide.

The victims aren't the only ones hurt by bullying. Bullying can also be dangerous for the bullies themselves. When bullies learn to get what they want through aggression and intimidation, they are setting themselves up for conflict and failure later in life.

What Is Bullying?

When a young person hurts a peer by regularly hitting, pushing, punching, or even just threatening him or her, it is physical bullying. Guys, take note: most physical bullies are boys. Boys are also more likely to be the victims of physical bullies than girls.

Other bullies don't need to use their hands to hurt. They insult their victims, call them names, taunt them, or talk behind their backs. This is called verbal bullying. It can feel just as bad as getting slapped or shoved.

There's also a third type of bullying: relationship bullying. That's when a group of people decides to exclude or pick on one person for no reason. It could mean refusing to spend time with a certain boy or giving him the silent treatment. It could mean making up rumors or lies about him. It could even mean forcing him to do something that makes him uncomfortable.

It's important to note that almost every kid experiments with making other people feel bad at some point. If you tease someone once, that doesn't make you a bully. And if another boy makes fun of you once, he's not necessarily bullying you. If the teasing and name-calling happen so regularly that it becomes a pattern, that's bullying.

Why Do Kids Bully?

When bullies know they can scare someone, make him cry, or force him to do something he doesn't want to do, they feel strong. When they can get other kids to gang up on someone, the bullies feel powerful. Bullies enjoy having power over others.

What kind of person is so desperate to feel powerful that he or she is willing to hurt other people? Often it is a person who secretly feels powerless or believes that he or

There are many reasons why boys become bullies. Some boys' families use threats, intimidation, or violence, and the bullies copy that behavior. Other boys think they need to bully to fit in.

she is threatened. Many bullies are incredibly insecure. A bully might be having trouble at home: maybe he doesn't get enough attention or love from his parents; maybe his relatives are violent, too. A bully might be ashamed that he can't keep up with other kids in school, so he bullies them to feel better about himself.

Some bullies make fun of others to deflect attention away from themselves. They believe that if they can make someone else a group's punching bag, they will escape teasing. Other bullies are angry because they are being bullied, perhaps by older kids, older siblings, or maybe even their own parents. These bullies want to vent their frustration and regain control of their lives by victimizing others as they were victimized.

Finally, there are bullies who just want to be macho. Too many boys think that being masculine means being tough, violent, intimidating, and powerful. Boys who feel insecure about their own masculinity, want to impress girls, or are anxious about their rank in popularity might think that bullying will prove that they are cool, tough, and manly.

What's So Bad About Bullying?

Bullying can have a huge impact on the life of the victim. The stress of being bullied can be so great that victims get distracted from their schoolwork or actually skip school altogether. In his book *Real Boys*, Dr. William Pollack writes that approximately 160,000 kids play hooky each day because they are afraid to go to school and face their bullies. Victims can become depressed and sad, withdraw from other people, and fantasize about revenge or suicide. They might even have trouble sleeping, digesting their food, and concentrating.

A 2003 National Education Association study found that bullying even affects kids who simply watch bullying happen. In schools where bullying is common, students learn less and are more likely to fear and disrespect each other.

Victims aren't the only ones who are hurt by bullying. In the long run, bullying is dangerous for the bullies. Some bullies eventually learn that it is wrong to hurt other people, and they change their bullying ways. But others never get the message. Bullies' aggression, risk-taking, and dedication to looking tough at any cost can seriously harm them later in life. A number of studies show that bullying is an early warning sign of other destructive behaviors. For example, a study by Dan Olweus found that by the time that middle school bullies reached age twenty-four, about 60 percent had been convicted of at least one crime. Teen bullies also had an increased risk of fighting, carrying a weapon, stealing, vandalizing, drinking, smoking, and dropping out of school.

What to Do If You Are Being Bullied

If you are being bullied, you are not alone. According to an article by Dr. Lori A. Sansone and Dr. Randy A. Sansone in the journal *Psychiatry*, approximately 10 percent of children and teens in the United States are the victims of bullying by peers.

Unfortunately, there is no one foolproof method for getting rid of a bully. Adults, teachers, and books like this can offer suggestions, but there is no guarantee that these ideas will completely solve the problem. That's just reality. That being said, if you are being bullied, the experts do have some tips that might make your life easier.

Being bullied might depress you or make you angry enough to turn your frustration on others. While you can't control how others treat you, you can control your own responses.

Risk Reduction

If a bully is threatening you with violence or roughing you up, stay out of that person's path. Figure out where the bully likes to spend time, and avoid those places. Go to school early or stay late. Stay with a group of students, or stay near a teacher or other adult. Try to avoid situations where you will be in an area all alone, like an empty locker room or playground. It may not be possible to stay out of the bully's way entirely. So if the bullying still persists, you need to know how to respond to it.

Changing Your Attitude

Do not assume that the bully will simply decide to stop. If he is having a good time bullying you now, he will continue until you change your reaction. A bully often makes a game out of trying to get a big reaction from you. Don't give him the satisfaction!

First, ignore the bully as much as possible. Pretend that the person doesn't exist. If ignoring the bully isn't an option, you can still try to rob him of a big reaction. Try as much as you can to hide that you are upset or hurt. When you answer the bully, stay strong, make eye contact, and keep your voice steady and clear. Practice funny comebacks. Act confident—even if you feel terrified.

However, do not try to trick yourself into thinking that you actually feel nothing. Don't bully yourself into deadening your emotions. You simply have to take your hurt and anger, put it aside, and deal with it at another time. Later, you can write about your feelings, talk to a friend, take out your anger on a punching bag, or express your emotions in another way. Just don't let the bully force you to panic in the moment.

Standing Up for Yourself

If you feel safe, you can try standing up for yourself. This doesn't mean you need to fight. Some people think that if

WHAT TO DO IF A CLASSMATE IS BEING BULLIED

What do you do if you see that a classmate is being bullied? You might be tempted to stand back and do nothing, telling yourself that it's none of your business or that you can't do anything to help. But when it comes to bullying, if you're not part of the solution, you are part of the problem. Bullies get away with terrorizing other kids because their classmates let them.

You can try to get the bully to stop with a few simple words. When you see him bullying someone, simply tell him to stop, grow up, or leave the victim alone. But you should only try this if you feel comfortable and safe speaking your mind to the bully.

As another option, you can report the bullying to a sympathetic adult like a parent, teacher, school nurse, or counselor. Make sure that you are as specific as possible, telling the adult exactly when, where, how, and why the bullying happened, in addition to who was involved.

Or you can simply reach out to the kid being bullied. Let the person know that you think he is being treated unfairly. Ask if he wants to talk about it. You will be amazed at how much better a little consideration and friendly support can make someone feel.

they beat the bully in a fight, the bullying will stop. It is more likely that a fight will provoke a mini-war and lead to more violence between the two sides. Besides, at some point every boy needs to learn how to stand up for himself nonviolently. Use words to tell the bully that you don't want to be treated this way and that you won't stand for it.

Learning how to stand up for yourself and insist on respect nonviolently is one of the most important parts of becoming a man.

Telling a Teacher

Let's face it: no one wants to tell an adult that they are being bullied. Many kids fear looking stupid or weak in an adult's eyes. They also don't want to be seen as a tattle-tale. Here's the thing, though: sometimes the only way to stop bullying behavior is to get an adult involved.

Telling isn't tattling, and it isn't being weak. It's just asking for help with something that most people can't handle on their own. If it's too painful to talk about how you are being bullied, write a letter. You don't have to tell a parent—any adult that you trust will do.

You're a Man After All

It takes bravery to admit what is going on and face your situation. And it takes real courage to avoid violence, even when the whole world is pressuring you to fight back. If you can stand up for yourself and declare that you are worthy of respect and consideration—without fighting—that's pretty tough. Anyone can get into a fight, but having the self-control, discipline, and courage to demand respect peacefully is really something special.

The experience of being bullied can be pretty painful. A lot of boys are left with anger and frustration after encounters with bullies. Whatever you do, don't take your negative feelings out on other people. You don't want to become a bully yourself!

What to Do If You Are a Bully

How can you tell if you are being a bully? After all, boys don't always pay close attention to others' feelings. And sometimes there's a thin line between joking and bullying. How do you know when a joke has gone too far?

The answer is simple: if you are intimidating others on purpose, and you know you can get away with it because you are bigger, stronger, or more popular, you are probably bullying. The next time that you feel like teasing, hitting, excluding, or being mean to someone, take a moment. Think about what it would be like to be in that person's shoes.

If you don't think you would feel hurt, take another moment. Be honest with yourself in considering how the other person might feel. Think about the last time someone really hurt your feelings. Remember how bad it felt. You have the power to keep someone else from feeling that way.

The ability to understand and share others' feelings is called empathy. A lot of bullies are actually lacking in empathy; they literally don't understand how their actions affect others. Psychologists call this "emotional illiteracy." Just as you can't get a good job if you don't know how to read and write, you can't build strong relationships with others if you have no empathy.

Empathy is a skill that can be learned. As a first step, start paying attention to your own emotions, no matter how scary or difficult they are. Notice how your feelings affect your voice, your body, and your facial expressions.

Next, study people's faces, tones of voice, and the way that they move. See if you can guess what emotional signals they are sending. Most people are actually pretty easy to read. Then, practice putting yourself in someone else's shoes, and imagine how he or she might feel in different situations.

Ask yourself why you think you push other kids around. What's making you so upset that you need to hurt others? What is stressing you out? Do you have problems that you are scared to look at or address directly? What do you think you are gaining from engaging in this behavior? Knowing why you are bullying can help you stop. Can you solve your problem in a positive way, instead of taking out your frustrations on innocent people? Can you vent your feelings in a way that doesn't hurt other kids? Can you feel powerful, successful, and popular without striking fear into the hearts of others?

A strong person does not need to bully, threaten, or intimidate others to earn respect. At the end of the day, making others feel good is actually much more satisfying than hurting them. The ultimate power is being able to act positively toward others without losing face yourself.

Ten Great Questions

to Ask a Guidance Counselor

1. What can I do to avoid or protect myself from bullies?

2. How can we decrease the amount of bullying and violence in our school?

3. How can I stand up for myself nonviolently?

4. Why do different people have different ideas about masculinity?

5. What should I do if my parents pressure me to express my masculinity in a certain way?

6. What do you think makes someone a real man?

7. Who are some positive male role models?

8. How can I keep my anger under control?

9. What do I do if my family doesn't understand me?

10. What do I do if I think I'll never fit in?

CHAPTER 3

Cyberbullying and Online Safety

The Internet can be a great thing. You can use it to do research for your homework and keep in touch with friends. You might have your own Facebook account for socializing. Maybe you have a blog or use instant messaging (IM), Twitter, or Tumblr. But the Internet has also created a whole new type of bullying: cyberbullying.

What Is Cyberbullying?

Simply put, cyberbullying is bullying on the Internet. When teens repeatedly insult, harass, humiliate, threaten, or torment each other online, it is cyberbullying.

In order to qualify as cyberbullying, the attacks typically must be repeated. If there is only one attack, it might count as cyberbullying, but only if the attack contains a clear and extremely frightening threat. Cyberbullying generally doesn't involve adults. When adults target children online, it is called cyberharassment or stalking. Here are some examples of cyberbullying:

Sending threatening texts or humiliating pictures to cell phones is one form of cyberbullying.

- A boy receives a series of threatening e-mails from an unfamiliar address, warning him that he's going to be beat up after school.

- A girl exchanges IMs with someone she thinks is a friend. The messages are actually from a group playing a mean practical joke on her.

- A group of students sets up a Web site dedicated to mocking and insulting an unpopular boy in their class.

- A boy gets his friends to post dozens of insults on a classmate's Facebook wall.

- A girl sends a sweet text message to a boy she likes, but he cruelly forwards the message on to everyone he knows so that they can make fun of her.

- A boy discovers that someone has been posing as him online. The person has been posting nasty rumors, racist comments, and other inappropriate things—all in his name!

- A boy forwards an embarrassing picture of a friend to his entire class.

Often, cyberbullies do not reveal their true identities online. They pose as someone else to write hateful things.

Sometimes they try to get their victim in trouble by borrowing the victim's identity and writing outrageous or offensive things online. Other times they might pose as a friend of the victim in order to win the victim's trust and then hurt his or her feelings.

Why Do Teens Cyberbully?

It's easy for bullies to hide their identities online, allowing them to bully without any consequences. Even if they do not hide their identities, bullies can be crueler on the Internet because they cannot see their victims' responses. It is easy to go too far, too fast.

Strangely, many cyberbullies are not bullies in person. In fact, kids who are bullied, beat up, teased, or humiliated at school might come home and transform into cyberbullies. Sometimes cyberbullies see themselves as giving the "real" bullies a taste of their own medicine.

If this sounds like you, remember that two wrongs don't make a right. "Real-life" bullies might seem powerful, confident, and carefree—but kids who are truly confident don't need to bully others. If you lash out at a bully online, you are probably hurting someone who is already troubled and sad. It is likely that your cyberbullying will make the bully-victim feel even angrier and more isolated, inspiring him to bully others even more in real life.

Prevention: Staying Safe Online

There are many hidden menaces on the Internet—from con men phishing (running online scams) to get your personal information to predators trying to contact lonely or

vulnerable kids. Unfortunately, many kids do not know how to use the Internet safely.

To protect yourself from cyberbullies, you must first learn basic online safety. First, only correspond online with people you know and like. If strangers or individuals with

Don't let cyberbullies push you into responding to them. Cyberbullies want to create drama online. When you refuse to play along, you rob them of their fun and keep your dignity.

whom you don't want contact write to you online, do not respond. If they keep trying to contact you, block them.

Even if you are taking the above precautions, you still need to be careful. Remember, you can't trust names and identities online. A person claiming to be a fourteen-year-old girl could easily be a fifty-year-old man. You can't even be sure that people who appear to be your friends online are your actual real-life friends. A person can pretend to be someone close to you in order to hurt you, confuse you, or trick you into embarrassing yourself or revealing valuable, private information.

Don't tell strangers anything about yourself online. Limit the amount of personal information you post on the Internet. And of course, you should never share any pictures or videos that you wouldn't want your parents to see—not through e-mail and not through text message or IM.

Cyberbullying and the Law

As technology transforms and makes new forms of bullying possible, the government is struggling to keep up. When the phenomenon of cyberbullying was first noticed, many states found themselves powerless to punish it because their laws did not yet cover the offense.

The tragedy of one young girl, Megan Meier of Dardenne Prairie, Missouri, has helped draw attention to the problem of cyberbullying. Megan was a bubbly thirteen-year-old volleyball player. She accepted a Myspace friend request from someone who claimed to be a boy named Josh Evans. He said he was new in town and was homeschooled. Megan and "Josh" became close online, but after a while, Josh turned on Megan and told her that he didn't want to be friends anymore. His messages got nastier. Eventually, Josh wrote to Megan, "The world would be a better place without you." Megan replied, "You're the kind of boy a girl would kill herself over." Twenty minutes later, Megan hung herself in her bedroom closet.

After Megan's death, it was discovered that "Josh" was actually the invention of an adult neighbor. Megan had a complicated friendship with the woman's thirteen-year-old daughter. The neighbor created the online character of Josh Evans to figure out what Megan thought about her daughter.

Megan's tragedy inspired the creation of a new Missouri state law, plus a pending federal law. The Megan Meier Cyberbullying Prevention Act would prevent communication "with the intent to coerce, intimidate, harass, or cause substantial emotional distress to a person, using electronic means to support severe, repeated, and hostile behavior." Other states are updating their antibullying laws to include cyberbullying. Current legal penalties for cyberbullying can vary from fines to jail time. Some school districts have adopted policies allowing them to punish students that cyberbully outside of school.

What to Do If You're Being Bullied Online

So what should you do if you're being bullied online? First of all, don't fight back. Many teens are tempted to write back to their tormenters to ask what they did wrong or to retaliate. This is exactly the wrong approach. When people send you mean messages or mock you online, it might seem like torture to sit back and do nothing. But cyberbullies want to provoke you. If you respond to them, you're giving them what they want!

When you realize you're being cyberbullied, immediately tell an adult you trust—no matter how embarrassing or painful the idea of "telling" might feel.

If someone is posing as you online, be sure to change your password and check your computer for viruses and hacks.

Next, tell a trusted adult. This might be difficult, embarrassing, or even painful to do, but it is necessary. First of

all, it's good for you to reach out to people who care about you. Too many victims of cyberbullying turn their anger on themselves, believing that it's their fault that they are being attacked. You need to be reminded that the whole world doesn't agree with the cyberbully. Second, an adult needs to know about the situation so that he or she can document and monitor it in case it gets out of hand.

If ignoring the cyberbully doesn't make him or her go away, you can take some concrete steps to keep the person from getting in touch with you. Block the person from contacting you via IM or e-mail. You can also send a warning notice or notify the bully's Internet service provider (ISP). Most ISPs ask their customers to agree to terms of service that prohibit harassment and cyberbullying. If the cyberbully gets enough warnings, he or she could lose access to the Internet or to the IM account through the ISP.

If the cyberbullying still persists, you have to go to the authorities. File a police report. You should also report the ISP of your cyberbully to your school. Even if the school's policies don't allow it to discipline the bully for something he or she wrote outside of school, administrators should know that one of their students is lashing out online.

Bullies Beware: The Dangers of Cyberbullying

Have you ever been tempted to treat someone cruelly online? If so, you need to realize that your actions will have consequences.

First and foremost, you are hurting another human being. Put yourself in your potential victim's shoes. Imagine how you would feel. Words, insults, taunts, and ostracism leave psychological scars that can last for years. Many victims of cyberbullying find it extremely difficult to trust other people again.

SUPPORTING BULLIED YOUTH ONLINE: THE IT GETS BETTER PROJECT

In September 2010, Dan Savage, an openly gay advice columnist and gay advocate, found himself disturbed and frustrated. He was constantly reading stories about gay teens who were "bullied to death"—that is, junior high and high school boys who committed suicide after being relentlessly teased and bullied about their sexual orientation. Savage realized that these teens couldn't imagine that their lives would ever get any better. He set out to prove them wrong by posting a YouTube video describing how he survived bullying and homophobia and went on to build a happy, successful, and fulfilling life.

Savage called his video message "It Gets Better," and he encouraged other people to share their own messages to gay, lesbian, bisexual, and transgendered youth. Soon more and more people were adding their own videos to the online project. Today, the It Gets Better Project includes videos from big names like President Barack Obama, Anne Hathaway, Joe Jonas, Ke$ha, Ellen DeGeneres, Colin Farrell, and many more. All of them were bullied or picked on in their youth, and all encourage teens who are being tormented to simply hold on, get past high school, and know that things will get better. The message is meant for outcast straight youth as well as gay teens.

The It Gets Better Project asks teens to take this pledge: "Everyone deserves to be respected for who they are. I pledge to spread this message to my friends, family and neighbors. I'll speak up against hate and intolerance whenever I see it, at school and at work. I'll provide hope for lesbian, gay, bi, trans, and other bullied teens by letting them know that 'It gets better.'"

Cyberbullying other people will likely come back to haunt you. Remember, the material that you post on the Internet now will never go away. One day, colleges and prospective employers will be able to look at every unprotected blog post, tweet, and Facebook status that you shared with the world. If you come off as cruel, crude, or stupid, it could have a serious impact on your future. If you go way too far, you could lose your access to the Internet, be suspended or expelled from school, or even face criminal charges.

CHAPTER 4

Managing Anger

Everyone has aggressive feelings sometimes. Everyone gets angry. However, part of growing up is learning how to manage your anger, control your aggressive urges, and resolve conflicts in a peaceful way.

It's funny: the Boy Code says that men aren't supposed to feel or show emotions. Anger is the one emotion that is totally acceptable for guys to express. If a guy throws a punch in anger, society might call him a hothead—but nobody will call him a sissy. According to this code, a guy doesn't need to be ashamed of feeling angry. As a result, a lot of boys focus more on their anger than on emotions like sadness or fear.

Unfortunately, anger can be a dangerous thing. If you are a person who carries around a lot of anger, you had better learn to control it. Otherwise, it will control you.

Before we begin, let's take one moment to acknowledge—well, really, debunk—one tenet of the Boy

Code. This code tells males that to prove their manhood, they have to fight. Disagreements can be stopped, points proved, or superiority settled by violence.

The truth is, violence is usually the absolute worst way to solve a conflict. It doesn't change anybody's mind, and it often leads to more violence.

When you allow your anger to boil over into violence, you put yourself and others in danger.

Fortunately, there are ways to resolve conflicts nonviolently, with honor. You can learn to use words instead of fists, and brains instead of brawn, to keep the peace. In the next two chapters, we'll talk about how to resolve conflicts peacefully, how to keep yourself from lashing out in anger, and how to make yourself less angry in general.

Anger: A Powerful Emotion

Anger gets a pretty bad rap. People think of it as a negative emotion—something to fear and avoid. Of course, anger can lead to violence, verbal abuse, fights, conflict, and drama. When people lose control of their anger, the results can be downright frightening, sometimes bloody, and often sad.

But there are some good things about anger, too. Anger can help you defend yourself or someone else. It can give you energy and inspire you to demand change. It can motivate you to improve yourself, work harder, and even become better at communicating.

Anger isn't good or bad; anger is a fact of life. Everyone experiences it. You can't eliminate anger from your life—but you can learn to use your anger in a positive way.

Think about anger as a tool, like a powerful jackhammer. If you point the jackhammer at other people, you'll hurt someone and get into a lot of trouble. If you throw yourself on the jackhammer in order to hide its motion and sound, you will hurt yourself. But if you learn to control the jackhammer, you can use it for something constructive and you don't need to be afraid of it. In other words, if you control your anger, it won't control you.

Understanding Anger

Like other emotions, anger affects the body as well as the brain. When you get angry, your body releases adrenaline. Your heart beats faster. Anger might make your face get hot and your chest feel tight. You might experience trouble breathing.

It's important to recognize that there are different types of anger. At the low end of the anger spectrum, you have irritation and annoyance. These are common emotions, and they are relatively easy to control. On the high end of the anger scale, you have extreme, blinding rage—anger so intense that it blocks out everything else.

In a perfect world, small irritations would annoy you just a little, and you would only get truly angry about big crimes and injustices. But life isn't always like that. Sometimes the smallest thing can cause someone to fly off the handle. Why is that?

Carrying Anger with You

Have you ever gotten really angry without quite understanding the reason why? Anger is a mysterious thing. Sometimes if you're really hurt or upset about something, but can't admit it, your emotions will come out in surprising ways. Maybe you'll get way too aggravated by your little sister. Or maybe you'll find yourself screaming at a teacher who asks you to be quiet in class.

When a small problem makes you lose control in a big way, chances are you are ignoring a larger problem in your life. You will probably keep getting upset about small things until you address the root of the problem.

Many adults who had difficult childhoods—distant parents, abuse, and other childhood traumas—end up having anger management issues later in life. For these people, the bigger problem is buried deep in the past. Until they face up to the pain they experienced as children, they often struggle with anger as adults.

What Do You Do with Anger?

Different people deal with anger in different ways. Some people give themselves over to rage, while others refuse to admit that they feel mad. Take a look at the following anger strategies, and ask yourself which one describes you.

Reacting Aggressively to Anger

This is the most dramatic way to react to anger. Many aggressive people let themselves get carried away by anger. They express it outwardly by yelling, screaming, hitting, or destroying property. Sometimes people take out their anger on somebody or something innocent, unfairly venting their rage.

Why do people lash out in anger? Well, it feels good in the moment. When you are acting out your anger, you get a jolt of adrenaline. You feel powerful. People may fear you. You may feel as if you have an excuse to do or say things that you normally wouldn't. You let out your emotions and get a little bit of relief from them.

Unfortunately, this relief doesn't last long. Too often, when the strong emotion of anger has passed, the person who lashed out has to deal with the consequences. These consequences could be as minor as hurt feelings or as serious as criminal arrest.

When you notice yourself starting to get really angry, stop in your tracks. Feel the anger, but count to ten before you decide how to act on your feelings.

Repressing Anger

Not everybody who experiences anger expresses it. Some people feel ashamed or afraid of their anger, so they deny that they are upset. They might not even admit their feelings to themselves. Perhaps they put on a false mask of cheerfulness, or they numb themselves so that they can't feel anything, positive or negative.

On the surface, this might seem like a smarter strategy than always expressing anger. After all, if you hide your anger, you can't get in trouble for it. However, repressing your anger—hiding it or pushing it away—also has consequences. Negative emotions do not go away if you repress them, or sweep them under the rug. If anything, they only grow stronger.

Emotions almost always find expression in some way. Repressed anger can lead people to abuse drugs and alcohol as they seek relief from the strength of their feelings. Bottling up anger might lead to depression or sudden outbursts of rage. In extreme cases, people who deny their anger might ultimately turn their frustration inward and mistreat or hurt themselves.

Being Assertive

Anger experts say that the correct and healthy response to anger is to be assertive. Don't deny your anger—allow yourself to experience it. Know that it is OK to be angry. Also know that anger is a passing emotion and you won't be angry forever.

Think about what is making you angry. Then, address the problem. Ask for what you want directly. Express your anger, but do it in a way that doesn't hurt or threaten anyone. Take responsibility for your actions, knowing that you are in charge of how you use your anger.

Getting Your Anger Under Control

Teaching yourself to become assertive takes self-control, discipline, thought, and practice over time. In the meantime, you can learn a few tricks that will help you get your anger under control.

Nip It in the Bud

The first trick is to notice when you first start getting angry. Feelings of anger often start with mild irritation or annoyance and then grow into more intense anger that is much harder to deal with. Try to notice when you get a little mad, then take steps to calm yourself down. It's much easier to put out a small fire than a three-alarm blaze!

To do this, first slow down. When people get angry, they naturally tense up. The tenser you become, the angrier you feel. When you notice yourself getting mad, slow down for a minute. Take some deep breaths. Try to relax your muscles. Many people find it helpful to count slowly to ten. When you slow yourself down, you can think through your next step more easily.

Anger management experts also recommend that you practice acting as if you were calm. You might not really be able to calm yourself down—you might feel extremely

angry. But you can still act calm. Try to behave in a calm manner until you feel your anger start to pass. It will be easier for you to figure out what to do next if you are clear-headed and relaxed.

Strategize

So you've caught yourself feeling irritated, and you've calmed yourself down. Now, instead of just acting out

Talking about your frustrations with friends can help you process your feelings and figure out what to do with your anger.

randomly, ask yourself a few questions. What just happened? Why did you get so angry? Was the event that set you off really a big deal? Are you actually under attack? Or are you overreacting?

Anger can be helpful when there is a true need to defend yourself. The problem is, many boys react to small insults like genuine attacks. A person stepping on your shoes should not provoke violence—even if he or she did it on purpose to upset you. Somebody calling you a name should not make you lash out—even if he or she did it to make you feel bad. When you lose your temper, you let the person teasing you win.

Assert Yourself

Eventually you need to learn to talk about how you feel and ask for what you want. While this step is more advanced, you can get to this point with practice.

Here's how to do it: Admit that you are angry, and explain why in a calm and respectful manner. Don't yell, don't scream, don't throw things, and don't insult anyone. Talk about how you feel using "I" words. For example, instead of shouting, "You stepped on my shoes, you jerk!" you could try saying, "When you keep stepping on my shoes, I feel really annoyed." This is less personal and less likely to sound like an attack on your adversary. Next, identify what would make you feel better and find a neutral way to ask for it. For instance, you might say, "This is the third time this week you've stepped on my shoes, so I guess you're doing it on purpose. If you have a problem with me, let's talk about it. But leave my shoes out of it."

Use Your Anger

Anger gives you energy, focus, and drive. One way to control your anger is to use that energy in a positive way.

Move around! A lot of boys find that running around, roughhousing, or playing sports is a great way to work

THE SEAL METHOD

Author Rosalind Wiseman created a system she calls SEAL for working out conflicts with friends. SEAL stands for:

1. Stop and strategize. Calm down, clear your mind, and think about the best way to solve your problem. Where should you talk to your opponent? At school? In the park? When will you do this? At lunchtime? After school? Over the weekend? What will you say? Wiseman says that even if you never get past this step, you have still improved your chances of avoiding violence and hurt feelings, just by taking a moment to think things through.

2. Explain. Tell the other person respectfully how you feel and why you got upset. Tell him or her how you want to be treated in the future. Be clear and concise.

3. Admit and affirm. Think about how you might have contributed to the conflict. Did you do anything to escalate the situation? Think about the situation from your opponent's point of view. Can you see the other person's side of the story? If so, admit that some of the things you did might have been out of line. Then, affirm that you have the right to be treated with respect.

THE SEAL METHOD CONTINUED

4. Lock. Wiseman says, "Lock the friendship in, lock it out, or take a vacation." Decide if this person needs to be in your life. If the answer is yes, tell the person that you still want to be friends. If the answer is no, tell him or her that you don't think you can be friends anymore. If you need some time to think things through, be honest about that, too.

out angry energy. In fact, anger can make you better at sports—more aggressive, more focused, and more determined. By the time that you're sweaty, you'll usually find that you are not so angry anymore.

If sports aren't your thing, any kind of physical activity will do. If you live in the country, chop some wood. If you live in the city, go for a walk. Focus your energy on building something or solving a problem. Clean up your room. Break down some cardboard boxes. Stay active and focused. Distract yourself until you feel your anger pass.

Self-expression might be one of the best methods of using your anger constructively. A lot of teens work out their anger by playing music. Bang loud on drums, play a guitar, or practice your violin. Channel your energy into playing. Practice your best heavy metal scream. Or just turn on your MP3 player and pump up your favorite song. Escape into the sound until your anger melts away.

If you find yourself obsessing over what made you angry, write down your feelings. Keep your thoughts in a secret journal or write a story about your angry feelings. Confessing how you feel on paper can be an incredible release. One important note: never blog or write on Facebook when you are really angry. It will come back to haunt you.

If you are good at visual art, draw a picture of how you feel. Express your anger in colors, lines, and symbols. Try to show the viewer exactly how you feel.

Or you can talk to a friend, a parent, a relative, or a teacher. Tell the person everything about how you feel. It might be difficult at first, but you will definitely feel relieved after getting your feelings off your chest. You might even get some good advice. The simple act of talking about your emotions can make you feel so much better.

As we discussed earlier, developing your sense of empathy for others can really help you control your anger. When people provoke you, treat you rudely, or are mean to you, try to put yourself in their shoes. It might be tough to do this, but if someone is treating you badly for no good reason, they probably feel pretty rotten inside. People generally hurt others because they are hurting themselves. Taking a moment to remember that can help quiet you down when you feel attacked or provoked.

Reflect on Your Anger

After your anger has passed, don't bury your feelings by denying that you ever got angry. Instead, examine the source of your anger. Think about why you got upset. If you became

agitated about something small, ask yourself if your anger was connected to something bigger. Are you frustrated by something in your life? Do you feel hurt, embarrassed, afraid, or disappointed? Why? What could fix the situation? You can only answer these questions by really experiencing your emotions. Don't be afraid of them. Think about them, and learn to analyze them and talk about them.

Vigorous exercise can calm you down when you're upset. Runners report that when they run for long periods, they experience a natural "runner's high" and feel happy and exhilarated.

Don't Beat Yourself Up

What if you are angry with yourself? How can you control your anger then? Everybody feels disappointed in themselves sometimes. Nobody is perfect, so don't beat yourself up about it. When you get angry at yourself, it is helpful to use the same steps that you would use with somebody else. Notice your anger. Feel it. Know that it will pass. Take deep breaths, relax, and calm yourself. Think about why you feel this way. Ask yourself what you can do to feel better. Can this feeling inspire you to improve or to try harder?

Above all, forgive yourself. Don't punish yourself by telling yourself how awful you are or by taking foolish risks. If you are thinking about hurting yourself in any way, talk to a trustworthy adult like a parent, teacher, or school counselor right away.

Myths and Facts

Myth

You should never feel angry.

Fact

Everybody feels angry sometimes. Anger can be a positive force when it motivates you to defend yourself, try harder, or demand change in an unfair situation. You cannot stop yourself from feeling anger—but you can make sure that you use anger in a constructive way.

Myth

You can get rid of anger by refusing to feel it.

Fact

You can't get rid of anger by simply denying that you are angry. If you pretend that you are not angry at all, your suppressed (held-in) anger will just build until you finally explode. It is far healthier to let yourself feel anger and then express it in a safe and peaceful way. Later, you can ask yourself why you got angry and whether you can change the circumstances that led to your anger.

Myths and Facts

Myth

Telling an adult that you're being bullied is tattling.

Fact

Tattling is telling on someone else when they've done something wrong that is minor. Telling an adult that you are being bullied is simply asking for help with a very serious problem. You don't need to be ashamed or reluctant to reach out for help. The best way to stop a bully is to tell a responsible adult.

CHAPTER 5

Preventing Anger and Practicing Nonviolence

It's normal to lose your temper every once in a while, especially when you are young. But some people actually make a habit of getting angry. Their anger feeds on itself. The more mad they get, the more unfair life seems to them and the more they find new things to get mad about. They become overwhelmed by their feelings, and it gets harder and harder for them to manage their negative emotions.

Don't get into the habit of getting angry. It is incredibly unhealthy to carry around a lot of anger. People who suffer from chronic anger might have trouble at school or at work. They might ruin their relationships and even develop health problems like high blood pressure, heart trouble, skin problems, and ulcers. It's very important for your brain and your body to learn how to deal with anger in a healthy way.

Tricks for Getting Less Angry

You have probably noticed that some people get a lot angrier than others. They might have a body that is very sensitive to stress. They might have an aggressive personality or come from an angry home. Maybe you are one of

Regular meditation can help you unwind and build confidence. Meditation can also help you see situations more clearly.

these people. Luckily, you can help yourself become less angry over time by taking a few simple steps.

Because anger is physical, you can actually decrease the amount of anger you feel by getting healthier. Make sure that you eat balanced meals. Cut down on the amount of caffeinated sodas and sugary foods you consume. Make sure that you get enough sleep; exhausted people often have a very short fuse.

You can also help yourself move past anger by trying time-honored techniques to calm yourself down. Practice relaxing yourself by learning to meditate. Clear your mind and breathe deeply. Count twenty breaths, breathing in and out slowly. When thoughts come into your head, try not to get wrapped up in them. Instead, observe them, watching your thoughts as if they were a movie. Let them come and go easily. Don't grab on to any one thought. If you feel yourself getting caught up in a thought, or obsessing, take a deep breath and let it go. Clear your mind and relax, again and again.

The more you practice meditation, the more helpful it becomes. When you get angry, you will have practice clearing your mind and relaxing.

Rehearse a Healthy Response

If you're the type of boy who likes to vent when you are really angry, it might be difficult at first to stop yourself from losing control. Luckily, practice makes perfect.

Before actors go onstage in front of hundreds of people, they rehearse—they decide how they will behave and practice behaving in that way. You can use the same technique to teach yourself to respond to anger in a positive way. Think about what makes you really furious. For instance, some boys hate to be teased. Other boys hate losing at sports. Some kids get really upset when someone talks down to them. These events are called "triggers" because they always provoke a response, setting your anger off almost automatically.

Think about what your trigger is. You might have more than one! Then, decide how you want to respond the next time you're faced with a trigger. Finally, you rehearse. Imagine that someone pushes your buttons; practice responding to that person in a self-controlled, mature way. Hopefully, the next time you are in a stressful situation, you'll be a little bit more prepared to recognize what is happening, control yourself, and respond the way you would like.

Some Ideas for Solving Conflicts Nonviolently

Perhaps the hardest part of anger management is learning to manage your anger during a fight. It's difficult to stay calm when you are being attacked. Anger is your body's natural response to aggression from others—it prepares you to fight back and defend yourself. But just because you feel like fighting doesn't mean you have to fight. For that matter, you don't have to fight just because that is what other people expect. Managing your anger means consciously deciding where, when, and how you will respond to insults, threats, and attacks.

If you are attacked or provoked, take a moment. Don't react reflexively, out of anger. If you have a serious problem with someone, don't try to deal with it while both of you are angry. Get out of the situation. Give the other person a chance to cool down, and approach him or her later.

Treat your opponent with respect. This might be challenging, but it's crucial. If you say that you want to work out a problem but treat your adversary disrespectfully, how can he or she trust you? Don't insult, belittle, or tease your

When you have a disagreement with someone, try to see things from that person's perspective. Admit your role in the conflict. Coming clean is a powerful way to move toward a peaceful resolution.

opponent. It's simple, but if you show respect, you will usually get more respect in return.

Can you listen to the other person? Can you figure out what you have in common with him or her? If you can

AGGRESSION IN ART

One of the best ways to work out aggression is through art. Countless men have found ways to express their aggression and turn it into something amazing.

Many styles of music make use of aggression. Punk rock was created in the 1970s as a way to express anger, rebelliousness, and plain old youthful exuberance. Refusing to conform to society's rules, punk rockers forged a style that shocked America, as well as a sound that genuinely frightened many members of polite society. Heavy metal musicians have expressed their aggressive feelings through insanely complex guitar licks, heavy drumming, and extreme speed. In hip-hop, artists use urgent and aggressive rhymes to express themselves.

Dance is often thought of as a feminine art form, but there are many ultra-masculine dance styles. At many rock shows, fans mosh by jumping around and slamming into each other. Then there's krumping, a form of freestyle, aggressive, fast break dancing that came out of South Central Los Angeles. Krumping developed as dancers competed with each other for supremacy. Other hip-hop dance styles like break dancing, turfing, and b-boying also feature aggressive moves and competition.

There are even painters who have used anger and aggression to bring their art to new levels. Abstract expressionist Willem de Kooning became famous for his aggressive brush strokes and chaotic paintings. Jackson Pollock was a very physical and aggressive painter who created his art by flinging, dripping, and splattering paint on his canvases. Former graffiti artist Jean-Michel

Basquiat created colorful, brash, and passionate images that almost leapt off their canvases.

In recent years, the sculptors and performance artists of Survival Research Laboratories have created sculptural robots that literally battle each other. Poets compete in poetry slams by performing their poems in urgent, tough, aggressive styles.

There are examples of aggressive art in every artistic medium. If you have an artistic bent, try expressing your feelings in art. You might surprise yourself with the passion and the quality of what you can produce.

pinpoint something that you share—for instance, neither one of you wants to fight and neither one of you wants to back out—you can point that out. Figure out what you can agree on.

Conclusion

Manhood means different things to different people. Our society's ideas about how men should act—what they should and shouldn't do, say, or feel—are changing all the time.

In the past, our society has had some pretty rigid ideas about what it means to be a man. Some of our culture's traditional masculine ideals are timeless, like strength (both physical and mental), responsibility, honor, respect, competition, and challenging yourself to achieve excellence.

But it's always possible to take a good thing too far. It's great to be powerful, but not when that means oppressing other people. It's wonderful to be respected, but not if you have to put down others to achieve that respect. It's

fantastic to feel like you belong, but not if that means changing who you are.

It can be dangerous for boys to emulate the masculine standard of the strong, silent man who never shows emotion. All people, men and women alike, feel emotions. No

Break dancing lets men all over the world express themselves through challenging and expressive movements. Above, members of Austria's BProdigy crew compete in France.

one is exempt. No one should be exempt! When you cut yourself off from emotions, you stop yourself from experiencing a big part of life. You numb yourself to joy as well as to sorrow. Emotions can and should be a source of strength, not a mark of shame.

Getting in touch with your feelings increases your ability to feel positive emotions like joy, pride, and excitement.

In today's information age, you need to communicate to succeed. If you cannot feel emotions, and you cannot empathize with others, you will not be a successful communicator. And if you can't communicate what you want, how can you connect with others and achieve your dreams? If you are ignoring or repressing all of your negative emotions, disappointments, and frustrations, how can you think clearly? How can you fulfill your potential?

The great thing is, you get to decide for yourself what kind of man you want to grow into. You get to decide how you want to live and how you want to define yourself. At the end of the day, becoming a man means becoming your true self.

GLOSSARY

adrenaline A substance released in the body, especially when one is excited, in danger, or in other high-stress situations. It makes the heart beat faster and allows the body to take in more oxygen.

adversary A person, group, or force that opposes or attacks; opponent.

aggression Angry or violent behavior or feelings.

assertive Confident and direct in claiming one's rights or expressing one's views.

Boy Code The set of beliefs and behaviors that boys expect of each other. The term was created by Dr. William S. Pollack.

bullying The act of repeatedly intimidating people, making them feel weak, excluding them from a group, or using violence to demonstrate their weakness. Bullying can be physical or verbal and can include turning a group against an individual or individuals.

chivalrous Following the medieval knightly code of chivalry, which included being polite, being brave, and being gallant and courteous to all women.

congregation An assembly of people brought together for religious worship.

cyberbullying Bullying that takes place over the Internet, cell phone, or any other form of electronic communication. Cyberbullying occurs between minors and is usually repeated.

demographic A section of the population sharing common characteristics, such as age, gender, income, etc.

depression A persistent and long-lasting state of mind that includes feeling down, hopeless, tired, and unmotivated.

effeminate Displaying qualities regarded as typical of a woman; not manly.

emotional intelligence The ability to understand and productively manage your own emotions, as well as the ability to recognize and sympathize with the emotions of others.

empathy The ability to understand and imaginatively share someone else's feelings.

fraternity A society of young men, usually found at colleges or universities. Many fraternities require young men to go through tests and ritual humiliations to prove that they deserve to join the group.

hazing The practice of subjecting newcomers to abusive or humiliating tricks, unnecessary or disagreeable tasks, and ridicule as part of an initiation process.

homophobia Fear of or prejudice against gay men, lesbians, bisexuals, transsexuals, and sometimes straight people who don't conform to traditional gender roles.

identity theft A crime in which criminals steal people's personal data in order to impersonate them, usually for financial gain.

Internet service provider (ISP) A company that allows customers to access the Internet.

masculine Having the qualities considered typical of or appropriate to a man; manly.

masculinity The quality or condition of being masculine.

meditation The act of clearing one's mind and practicing quiet mindfulness in order to relax and focus. Meditation is sometimes, but not always, a spiritual or religious activity.

nonviolence Avoidance of violence.

ostracize To banish or exclude a person from a group.

paranoia Excessive suspicion of the motives of others.

passive-aggressive Displaying behavior in which one lashes out in an unassertive manner, for example by dragging one's feet in cooperating with people, refusing to communicate, etc.

prejudice A negative belief or opinion that is based on received knowledge, not personal observation or experience.

provoke To excite to anger or violence.

reflexive Characterized by behavior that is done automatically or habitually, without thinking, as a reaction to something.

relationship bullying Bullying by excluding someone from a group or influencing the people around a person to make him an outcast.

repress To unconsciously refuse to feel or think certain thoughts, emotions, memories, or impulses so that they never reach the waking mind.

retaliate To strike back at somebody after being attacked, often in a way that copies the original attack.

strategize To plan out something consciously and deliberately in advance.

suppress The conscious decision to put a thought, emotion, memory, or impulse out of one's mind.

Big Brothers Big Sisters of America
230 North 13th Street
Philadelphia, PA 19107
(215) 567-7000
Web site: http://www.bbbs.org
This organization pairs young people with adult volunteers who offer them one-on-one guidance. It is a great way for boys to connect with positive, caring, and safe male role models.

Big Brothers Big Sisters of Canada
Les Grands Frères Grandes Soeurs du Canada
3228 South Service Road, Suite 113E
Burlington, ON L7N 3H8
Canada
(800) 263-9133
Web site: http://www.bigbrothersbigsisters.ca
This popular mentoring organization pairs kids and teens with grown-up volunteers to help guide and counsel them.

Boys to Men
565 Congress Street
Room 206A
Portland, ME 04101
(207) 774-9994
Web site: http://www.boystomen.info
The mission of this organization is to reduce interpersonal violence by offering programs that support the healthy development of adolescent boys. Boys to Men envisions a world in

which all boys have the opportunity to develop into healthy men, supported by adult mentors who model healthy masculinity and respectful, nonviolent relationships.

Center for the Study and Prevention of Violence (CSPV)

Institute of Behavioral Science
University of Colorado at Boulder
483 UCB
Boulder, CO 80309
(303) 492-1032
Web site: http://www.colorado.edu/cspv

CSPV was founded in 1992 to provide informed assistance to groups committed to understanding and preventing violence, particularly adolescent violence. The center works to establish more complete and valuable information to impact violence-related policies, programs, and practices.

Office of Safe and Drug-Free Schools (OSDFS)

550 12th Street SW, 10th Floor
Washington, DC 20202-6450
(202) 245-7896
Web site: http://www2.ed.gov/about/offices/list/osdfs

Among other important functions, this U.S. government office coordinates school programs and activities that promote health and character education and prevent violence and drug use.

PREVNet

PREVNet Administrative Centre
Queen's University

98 Barrie Street
Kingston, ON K7L 3N6
Canada
(613) 533-2632
Web site: http://www.prevnet.ca

PREVNet is a Canadian network of government offices, researchers, and nongovernmental organizations (NGOs) working together to stop bullying.

STRYVE
Centers for Disease Control and Prevention
4770 Buford Highway, NE MS F-64
Atlanta, GA 30341
(800) CDC-INFO [232-4636]
Web site: http://www.safeyouth.gov

STRYVE, or Striving To Reduce Youth Violence Everywhere, is a national initiative led by the Centers for Disease Control and Prevention (CDC) to prevent youth violence before it starts among young people ages ten to twenty-four. STRYVE's vision is safe and healthy youth who can achieve their full potential as connected and contributing members of thriving, violence-free families, schools, and communities.

Students Against Violence Everywhere (SAVE)
National Association of SAVE
322 Chapanoke Road, Suite 110
Raleigh, NC 27603
(866) 343-SAVE
Web site: http://www.nationalsave.org

SAVE helps teens educate each other and their communities about the consequences of violence and how to use nonviolence in everyday life.

The Trevor Project
Administrative Offices
8704 Santa Monica Boulevard, Suite 200
West Hollywood, CA 90069
(310) 271-8845 (office); (866) 4-U-TREVOR (hotline)
Web site: http://www.thetrevorproject.org

This organization is dedicated to ending suicide among gay, lesbian, bisexual, and transsexual teens. The Trevor Project offers a twenty-four-hour hotline and an online community and advice column.

Young Men's Health
Children's Hospital Boston
333 Longwood Avenue, 5th Floor
Boston, MA 02115
Web site: http://www.youngmenshealthsite.org

This organization helps teen boys improve their understanding of normal health and development (including emotional health), as well as of specific diseases and conditions.

Web Sites

Due to the changing nature of Internet links, Rosen Publishing has developed an online list of Web sites related to the subject of this book. This site is updated regularly. Please use this link to access the list:

http://www.rosenlinks.com/ymg/mba

FOR FURTHER READING

Canada, Geoffrey, and Jamar Nicholas. *Fist, Stick, Knife, Gun: A Personal History of Violence in America.* Boston, MA: Beacon Press, 2010.

Drew, Naomi. *Working Out Conflicts: How to Keep Cool, Stay Safe, and Get Along*. Minneapolis, MN: Free Spirit, 2004.

Ehrman, M. K. *Just Chill: Navigating Social Norms and Expectations* (Guy's Guide). Edina, MN: ABDO Publishing, 2011.

Harper, Hill. *Letters to a Young Brother: Manifest Your Destiny.* New York, NY: Gotham Books, 2006.

Hayhurst, Chris. *Stay Cool: A Guy's Guide to Handling Conflict*. New York, NY: Rosen Publishing, 2000.

McCollum, Sean. *Managing Conflict Resolution* (Character Education). New York, NY: Chelsea House, 2009.

McKay, Brett, and Kate McKay. *The Art of Manliness: Classic Skills and Manners for the Modern Man.* Cincinnati, OH: HOW Books, 2009.

Mikaelson, Ben. *Ghost of Spirit Bear*. New York, NY: Scholastic, 2010.

Miller, Karen. *Male and Female Roles* (Opposing Viewpoints). Farmington Hills, MI: Greenhaven Press, 2010.

Monteverde, Matt. *Making Smart Choices About Violence, Gangs, and Bullying*. New York, NY: Rosen Publishing, 2008.

Nagle, Jeanne. *GLBT Teens and Society* (Teens: Being Gay, Lesbian, Bisexual, or Transgender). New York, NY: Rosen Publishing, 2010.

Pitt, Steve. *Guyness: Deal with It Body and Soul*. Toronto, Canada: James Lorimer, 2005.

Quill, Charlie. *Anger and Anger Management*. New York, NY: Rosen Publishing, 2009.

Shapiro, Ouisie. *Bullying and Me: Schoolyard Stories*. Chicago, IL: Albert Whitman & Company, 2010.

Woodward, John. *Men and Masculinity* (Opposing Viewpoints). Farmington Hills, MI: Greenhaven Press, 2010.

BIBLIOGRAPHY

Biddulph, Steve. *Raising Boys: Why Boys Are Different—and How to Help Them Become Happy and Well-Balanced Men*. 2nd ed. Berkeley, CA: Celestial Arts, 2008.

Canada, Geoffrey. *Reaching Up for Manhood: Transforming the Lives of Boys in America*. Boston, MA: Beacon Press, 1998.

Centers for Disease Control and Prevention. "Youth Violence: Facts at a Glance." 2010. Retrieved March 8, 2011 (http://www.cdc.gov/violenceprevention/pdf/YV-FactSheet-a.pdf).

Department of Health and Human Services. "What Is Bullying?" Retrieved March 8, 2011 (http://www.stopbullyingnow.hrsa.gov/topics/what_is_bullying).

Education.com. "Bullying Information Center." Retrieved March 8, 2011 (http://www.education.com/topic/school-bullying-teasing).

Garbarino, James. *Lost Boys: Why Our Sons Turn Violent and How We Can Save Them*. New York, NY: Free Press, 1999.

Gentry, W. Doyle. *Anger Management for Dummies*. Hoboken, NJ: Wiley Publishing, 2007.

It Gets Better Project. "What Is the It Gets Better Project?" Retrieved March 8, 2011 (http://www.itgetsbetter.org/pages/about-it-gets-better-project).

Kimmel, Michael S. *Guyland: The Perilous World Where Boys Become Men*. New York, NY: Harper, 2008.

Kindlon, Dan, and Michael Thompson. *Raising Cain: Protecting the Emotional Life of Boys*. New York, NY: Ballantine Books, 1999.

Liptak, John J., and Ester A. Leutenberg. *The Anger & Aggression Workbook: Self-Assessments, Exercises, & Educational Handouts*. Duluth, MN: Whole Person Associates, 2008.

Lohmann, Raychelle Cassada. *The Anger Workbook for Teens: Activities to Help You Deal with Anger and Frustration*. Oakland, CA: Instant Help Books, 2009.

Marshall, Joseph, and Lonnie Wheeler. *Street Soldier: One Man's Struggle to Save a Generation, One Life at a Time*. New York, NY: Delacorte Press, 1996.

Mental Health America. "Bullying and Gay Youth." 2011. Retrieved March 8, 2011 (http://www.nmha.org/go/information/get-info/children-s-mental-health/bullying-and-gay-youth).

Morrill, Donald. *Sounding for Cool*. East Lansing, MI: Michigan State University Press, 2002.

National Crime Prevention Council. "Cyberbullying." 2011. Retrieved March 8, 2011 (http://www.ncpc.org/cyberbullying).

PBS.org. "It's My Life: Friends: Bullies." 2005. Retrieved March 8, 2011 (http://pbskids.org/itsmylife/friends/bullies).

PBS.org. "Understanding and Raising Boys." 2011. Retrieved March 8, 2011 (http://www.pbs.org/parents/raisingboys).

TeensHealth. "Dealing with Bullying." 2011. Retrieved March 8, 2011 (http://kidshealth.org/teen/your_mind/problems/bullies.html).

Thompson, Michael, and Teresa Barker. *Speaking of Boys: Answers to the Most-Asked Questions About Raising Sons*. New York, NY: Ballantine Books, 2000.

TrueChild. "Masculinity and Bullying." 2011. Retrieved March 8, 2011 (http://www.truechild.org/PageDisplay.asp?p1=6280).

WiredKids, Inc. "STOP Cyberbullying: Cyberbullying—What It Is, How It Works, and How to Understand and Deal with Cyberbullies." Retrieved March 8, 2011 (http://www.stopcyberbullying.org/index2.html).

Wiseman, Rosalind. *Queen Bees & Wannabes*. New York, NY: Crown Publishers, 2002.

A

B

C